STAR WARS®

THE CLONE WARS™
MAD LIBS®

by Roger Price and Leonard Stern

PSS!
PRICE STERN SLOAN

PRICE STERN SLOAN
Published by the Penguin Group
Penguin Group (USA) Inc., 375 Hudson Street, New York, New York 10014, USA
Penguin Group (Canada), 90 Eglinton Avenue East, Suite 700,
Toronto, Ontario M4P 2Y3, Canada
(a division of Pearson Penguin Canada Inc.)
Penguin Books Ltd., 80 Strand, London WC2R 0RL, England
Penguin Group Ireland, 25 St. Stephen's Green, Dublin 2, Ireland
(a division of Penguin Books Ltd.)
Penguin Group (Australia), 250 Camberwell Road, Camberwell, Victoria 3124, Australia
(a division of Pearson Australia Group Pty. Ltd.)
Penguin Books India Pvt. Ltd., 11 Community Centre,
Panchsheel Park, New Delhi—110 017, India
Penguin Group (NZ), 67 Apollo Drive, Rosedale, North Shore 0632, New Zealand
(a division of Pearson New Zealand Ltd.)
Penguin Books (South Africa) (Pty.) Ltd., 24 Sturdee Avenue,
Rosebank, Johannesburg 2196, South Africa

Penguin Books Ltd., Registered Offices:
80 Strand, London WC2R 0RL, England

This book is published in partnership with LucasBooks, a division of Lucasfilm Ltd.

Mad Libs format copyright © 2009 by Price Stern Sloan.

Published by Price Stern Sloan,
a division of Penguin Young Readers Group,
345 Hudson Street, New York, New York 10014.

ISBN 978-0-8431-3357-8

7 9 10 8

MAD LIBS

INSTRUCTIONS

MAD LIBS® is a game for people who don't like games!
It can be played by one, two, three, four, or forty.

• RIDICULOUSLY SIMPLE DIRECTIONS

In this tablet you will find stories containing blank spaces where words are
left out. One player, the READER, selects one of these stories. The READER
does not tell anyone what the story is about. Instead, he/she asks the other
players, the WRITERS, to give him/her words. These words are used to fill
in the blank spaces in the story.

• TO PLAY

The READER asks each WRITER in turn to call out words—an adjective or
a noun or whatever the space calls for—and uses them to fill in the blank
spaces in the story. The result is a MAD LIBS® game.

When the READER then reads the completed MAD LIBS® game to the
other players, they will discover that they have written a story that is
fantastic, screamingly funny, shocking, silly, crazy, or just plain dumb—
depending upon which words each WRITER called out.

• EXAMPLE (Before and After)

" _____ !" he said _____
EXCLAMATION   ADVERB

as he jumped into his convertible _____ and
                                            NOUN

drove off with his _____ wife.
                          ADJECTIVE

" _____Ouch_____ !" he said _____stupidly_____
       EXCLAMATION   ADVERB

as he jumped into his convertible _____cat_____ and
                                          NOUN

drove off with his _____brave_____ wife.
                          ADJECTIVE

MAD LIBS

QUICK REVIEW

In case you have forgotten what adjectives, adverbs, nouns, and verbs are, here is a quick review:

An **ADJECTIVE** describes something or somebody. *Lumpy, soft, ugly, messy,* and *short* are adjectives.

An **ADVERB** tells how something is done. It modifies a verb and usually ends in "ly." *Modestly, stupidly, greedily,* and *carefully* are adverbs.

A **NOUN** is the name of a person, place, or thing. *Sidewalk, umbrella, bridle, bathtub,* and *nose* are nouns.

A **VERB** is an action word. *Run, pitch, jump,* and *swim* are verbs. Put the verbs in past tense if the directions say PAST TENSE. *Ran, pitched, jumped,* and *swam* are verbs in the past tense.

When we ask for **A PLACE**, we mean any sort of place: a country or city *(Spain, Cleveland)* or a room *(bathroom, kitchen).*

An **EXCLAMATION** or SILLY WORD is any sort of funny sound, gasp, grunt, or outcry, like *Wow!, Ouch!, Whomp!, Ick!,* and *Gadzooks!*

When we ask for specific words, like a **NUMBER**, a COLOR, an **ANIMAL**, or a PART OF THE BODY, we mean a word that is one of those things, like *seven, blue, horse,* or *head.*

When we ask for a **PLURAL**, it means more than one. For example, *cat* pluralized is *cats.*

MAD LIBS® is fun to play with friends, but you can also play it by yourself! To begin with, DO NOT look at the story on the page below. Fill in the blanks on this page with the words called for. Then, using the words you have selected, fill in the blank spaces in the story.

Now you've created your own hilarious MAD LIBS® game!

WATCHING ANAKIN GROW UP, BY OBI-WAN KENOBI

NOUN _____

ADJECTIVE _____

ADJECTIVE _____

PLURAL NOUN _____

ADJECTIVE _____

NOUN _____

NOUN _____

ADVERB _____

ADJECTIVE _____

NOUN _____

ADJECTIVE _____

ADJECTIVE _____

ADVERB _____

ADJECTIVE _____

NOUN _____

PART OF THE BODY _____

MAD LIBS
WATCHING ANAKIN GROW UP, BY OBI-WAN KENOBI

When I first met Anakin, he was no more than a little

_____. He was very Force-sensitive, but he seemed
    NOUN

too _____ to become a Jedi Knight. Boy, was I
    ADJECTIVE

_____! In just a few short _____, Anakin
  ADJECTIVE   PLURAL NOUN

has proven himself to be a/an _____ Jedi _____.
                      ADJECTIVE   NOUN

Now he's even training his own _____. He may be a
                 NOUN

reluctant teacher, but he is doing it _____. He and his
               ADVERB

_____ Padawan, Ahsoka, fight side by _____ like
  ADJECTIVE   NOUN

they've been doing it for years. They also know how to laugh with

each other, which is important for building a/an _____
                                      ADJECTIVE

relationship between Master and learner. In every task he's taken

on in the Clone Wars, Anakin's been brave and _____.
                                      ADJECTIVE

I am _____ lucky to teach him and to learn from him.
    ADVERB

One day, I'm sure he'll be the most _____ Jedi in the entire
                           ADJECTIVE

_____. (But let's just keep that between us. We don't want
  NOUN

his _____ getting too big!)
  PART OF THE BODY

MAD LIBS® is fun to play with friends, but you can also play it by yourself! To begin with, DO NOT look at the story on the page below. Fill in the blanks on this page with the words called for. Then, using the words you have selected, fill in the blank spaces in the story.

Now you've created your own hilarious MAD LIBS® game!

AHSOKA,
THE AWESOME PADAWAN

ADJECTIVE _____

ADJECTIVE _____

NOUN _____

PART OF THE BODY _____

ADJECTIVE _____

NOUN _____

EXCLAMATION _____

VERB ENDING IN "ING" _____

ADJECTIVE _____

PERSON IN ROOM _____

PART OF THE BODY (PLURAL) _____

ADJECTIVE _____

ADVERB _____

NOUN _____

MAD LIBS
AHSOKA,
THE AWESOME PADAWAN

Anakin Skywalker's new _____ Padawan, Ahsoka,
                              ADJECTIVE

might be smaller and more _____ than your average
                                    ADJECTIVE

_____, but she's got more _____ than
     NOUN   PART OF THE BODY

ten Jedi Masters put together. Not only is she brave, she's smart as

well. She can solve any _____ problem at the speed
                             ADJECTIVE

of _____. And, _____, is she fast with a
       NOUN   EXCLAMATION

lightsaber. When she's _____ against a battle droid
                    VERB ENDING IN "ING"

or the _____ General _____, it's hard to
       ADJECTIVE   PERSON IN ROOM

take your _____ off her. Ahsoka might be young
       PART OF THE BODY (PLURAL)

and she might be _____, but she always gets the job
               ADJECTIVE

done _____. There's no doubt about it—she's a rising
      ADVERB

_____!
   NOUN

MAD LIBS® is fun to play with friends, but you can also play it by yourself! To begin with, DO NOT look at the story on the page below. Fill in the blanks on this page with the words called for. Then, using the words you have selected, fill in the blank spaces in the story.

Now you've created your own hilarious MAD LIBS® game!

BEING A CLONE COMMANDER, BY REX

NOUN _____

PLURAL NOUN _____

PLURAL NOUN _____

ADJECTIVE _____

ADJECTIVE _____

NUMBER _____

NOUN _____

VERB ENDING IN "ING" _____

ADJECTIVE _____

VERB ENDING IN "ING" _____

PLURAL NOUN _____

VERB ENDING IN "ING" _____

NOUN _____

PART OF THE BODY _____

ADJECTIVE _____

ADJECTIVE _____

ADVERB _____

NOUN _____

So you'd like to lead a squadron of _____ troopers? Well, it's

NOUN

not all fun and _____ fighting the bad _____;

PLURAL NOUN   PLURAL NOUN

it's also really _____ work. For one thing, you

ADJECTIVE

always have to be on your game, on the lookout for anything

_____ 24-_____. You're on call morning,

ADJECTIVE   NUMBER

noon, and _____. You might be _____

NOUN   VERB ENDING IN "ING"

peacefully, when suddenly your Jedi Knight's _____

ADJECTIVE

voice comes _____ out of nowhere commanding

VERB ENDING IN "ING"

you to battle _____ immediately. When you've

PLURAL NOUN

been _____ in battles as long as I have, you learn

VERB ENDING IN "ING"

three very important things. First thing to remember: The

_____ always comes first. Second, if you get captured,

NOUN

keep your _____ shut. Third, and most _____,

PART OF THE BODY   ADJECTIVE

experience outranks everything. Keep these three _____

ADJECTIVE

things in mind, and your squadron will _____ respect

ADVERB

your _____.

NOUN

MAD LIBS® is fun to play with friends, but you can also play it by yourself! To begin with, DO NOT look at the story on the page below. Fill in the blanks on this page with the words called for. Then, using the words you have selected, fill in the blank spaces in the story.

Now you've created your own hilarious MAD LIBS® game!

C-3PO TO THE RESCUE

NOUN _____

NOUN _____

ADJECTIVE _____

ADJECTIVE _____

PLURAL NOUN _____

NOUN _____

PLURAL NOUN _____

ADJECTIVE _____

ADJECTIVE _____

VERB ENDING IN "ING" _____

PLURAL NOUN _____

PLURAL NOUN _____

ADJECTIVE _____

C-3PO TO THE RESCUE

He might move as slow as a/an _____, but when push
NOUN

comes to _____, C-3PO really pulls through for you.
NOUN

During the _____ Clone Wars, he came to the rescue
ADJECTIVE

whenever Padmé was in _____ trouble. It was 3PO
ADJECTIVE

who gathered a group of clone _____, stormed the
PLURAL NOUN

_____, and saved Padmé from the _____
NOUN   PLURAL NOUN

of the _____ Ziro the Hutt. And, as reluctant as he
ADJECTIVE

might have been to go in after Padmé at the _____
ADJECTIVE

Rodian Consulate with Jar Jar Binks, he did it anyway, and because

of his clever _____, he was able to make contact with
VERB ENDING IN "ING"

Republic _____ who saved them all from certain doom!
PLURAL NOUN

One thing's for sure when it comes to 3PO—_____
PLURAL NOUN

can be deceiving! He might not look like a/an _____
ADJECTIVE

hero, but he can't help being one!

FROM STAR WARS®: THE CLONE WARS™ MAD LIBS® • Copyright © 2009 Lucasfilm Ltd. & ® or ™ where
indicated. All Rights Reserved. Used Under Authorization. Published by Price Stern Sloan, a division of
Penguin Young Readers Group, 345 Hudson Street, New York, NY 10014.

MAD LIBS® is fun to play with friends, but you can also play it by yourself! To begin with, DO NOT look at the story on the page below. Fill in the blanks on this page with the words called for. Then, using the words you have selected, fill in the blank spaces in the story.

Now you've created your own hilarious MAD LIBS® game!

JABBA ON THE JEDI, TRANSLATED FROM HUTTESE

ADJECTIVE _____

PLURAL NOUN _____

VERB ENDING IN "ING" _____

ADJECTIVE _____

PLURAL NOUN _____

NOUN _____

ADJECTIVE _____

NOUN _____

ADJECTIVE _____

COLOR _____

PLURAL NOUN _____

MAD LIBS
JABBA ON THE JEDI,
TRANSLATED FROM HUTTESE

The galaxy would be a/an _____ place if we could
ADJECTIVE

just rid it of these Jedi and Sith _____ once and for
PLURAL NOUN

all. They're always _____ among themselves and
VERB ENDING IN "ING"

creating _____ problems for the rest of us. I've had
ADJECTIVE

it up to here with their endless _____. And somehow,
PLURAL NOUN

even though I mind my own _____, I always end up
NOUN

getting involved. This time, the Jedi and the Sith have made me really

_____. To think that they would kidnap my pride and
ADJECTIVE

_____—my _____ son, Rotta—and hold
NOUN   ADJECTIVE

him for ransom has me seeing _____. I don't care what
COLOR

they do to each other—just leave me and my _____
PLURAL NOUN

out of it!

MAD LIBS® is fun to play with friends, but you can also play it by yourself! To begin with, DO NOT look at the story on the page below. Fill in the blanks on this page with the words called for. Then, using the words you have selected, fill in the blank spaces in the story.

Now you've created your own hilarious MAD LIBS® game!

WHAT I'VE LEARNED FROM THE CLONE WARS, BY ANAKIN SKYWALKER

ADJECTIVE _____

ADJECTIVE _____

ADJECTIVE _____

NOUN _____

PLURAL NOUN _____

ADJECTIVE _____

NOUN _____

ADJECTIVE _____

PLURAL NOUN _____

PLURAL NOUN _____

VERB ENDING IN "ING" _____

ADJECTIVE _____

MAD LIBS

WHAT I'VE LEARNED FROM THE CLONE WARS, BY ANAKIN SKYWALKER

The Clone Wars have been _____ and dangerous, but
                              ADJECTIVE

through it all, I've learned some very _____ lessons:
                                          ADJECTIVE

1. Never lose your _____ astromech droid, especially
                      ADJECTIVE

when said droid is your _____ *and* his memory is full
                            NOUN

of battle _____ and other Republic secrets.
              PLURAL NOUN

2. Big surprises can come in _____ packages. When I
                                ADJECTIVE

first met Ahsoka, I thought she was nothing more than a snippy little

_____, but she's proved herself to be a/an _____
     NOUN   ADJECTIVE

partner in the fight against the Separatist _____.
                                                PLURAL NOUN

3. Be careful which _____ you trust and confide in.
                        PLURAL NOUN

You never know who is _____ for the other side.
                          VERB ENDING IN "ING"

This includes _____ droids.
                  ADJECTIVE

MAD LIBS® is fun to play with friends, but you can also play it by yourself! To begin with, DO NOT look at the story on the page below. Fill in the blanks on this page with the words called for. Then, using the words you have selected, fill in the blank spaces in the story.

Now you've created your own hilarious MAD LIBS® game!

ANAKIN'S GUIDE TO TRAINING A PADAWAN

PART OF THE BODY _____

ADJECTIVE _____

ADJECTIVE _____

ADJECTIVE _____

ADVERB _____

PART OF THE BODY (PLURAL) _____

ADJECTIVE _____

VERB _____

ADJECTIVE _____

ADJECTIVE _____

ADJECTIVE _____

When Ahsoka told me that Master Yoda wanted me to train her, my

_____ dropped to the floor. Obi-Wan could say all he
PART OF THE BODY

wanted about what a/an _____ privilege it is to teach,
ADJECTIVE

but I knew the truth—a/an _____ Padawan would
ADJECTIVE

only slow me down. But since I didn't have any choice in the matter,

I began to train the _____ Ahsoka. To tell you the truth
ADJECTIVE

I'm _____ enjoying it. I've been training her the only
ADVERB

way I know how: through _____-on experience.
PART OF THE BODY (PLURAL)

During a war, there's no time to learn from _____
ADJECTIVE

books—it's a/an _____ or swim situation. I'm proud
VERB

to say that Ahsoka has surpassed all our _____
ADJECTIVE

expectations. She may look like a/an _____ youngling,
ADJECTIVE

but she fights like a/an _____ Jedi Master.
ADJECTIVE

MAD LIBS® is fun to play with friends, but you can also play it by yourself! To begin with, DO NOT look at the story on the page below. Fill in the blanks on this page with the words called for. Then, using the words you have selected, fill in the blank spaces in the story.

Now you've created your own hilarious MAD LIBS® game!

ASAJJ VENTRESS'S GUIDE TO LIGHTSABER DUELING

PART OF THE BODY _____

NOUN _____

ADJECTIVE _____

NOUN _____

ADJECTIVE _____

ADVERB _____

PLURAL NOUN _____

PLURAL NOUN _____

VERB ENDING IN "ING" _____

ADJECTIVE _____

PART OF THE BODY _____

PLURAL NOUN _____

NOUN _____

PART OF THE BODY _____

If you ever find yourself face-to-_____ with a
PART OF THE BODY

despicable Jedi _____ in a lightsaber duel, remember
NOUN

these _____ tips and tricks:
ADJECTIVE

1. The element of surprise is always your best _____.
NOUN

I'll never forget the look of shock on Ahsoka's _____
ADJECTIVE

face when I _____ attacked out of nowhere.
ADVERB

2. Why use a lightsaber with only one blade when you can get one

with two _____? After all, two _____ are
PLURAL NOUN _PLURAL NOUN_

better than one!

3. When _____ with your enemies, always keep
VERB ENDING IN "ING"

them talking. It's a/an _____ way to gain the upper
ADJECTIVE

_____.
PART OF THE BODY

4. Always travel with an army of super battle _____.
PLURAL NOUN

You never know when you'll need a/an _____ to cover
NOUN

your _____.
PART OF THE BODY

MAD LIBS® is fun to play with friends, but you can also play it by yourself! To begin with, DO NOT look at the story on the page below. Fill in the blanks on this page with the words called for. Then, using the words you have selected, fill in the blank spaces in the story.

Now you've created your own hilarious MAD LIBS® game!

THE LIFE OF A CLONE TROOPER

ADJECTIVE _____

NOUN _____

ADJECTIVE _____

NOUN _____

PLURAL NOUN _____

NOUN _____

NOUN _____

NOUN _____

ADJECTIVE _____

PLURAL NOUN _____

PLURAL NOUN _____

ADJECTIVE _____

NOUN _____

ADVERB _____

VERB _____

TYPE OF LIQUID _____

PART OF THE BODY _____

MAD LIBS

THE LIFE OF A CLONE TROOPER

The life of a clone trooper is a/an _____ one. A clone
                                         ADJECTIVE

trooper wakes up every morning at the crack of _____.
                                                   NOUN

After eating a/an _____ breakfast of _____
                     ADJECTIVE   NOUN

and _____, the day's work begins. Whether it's
        PLURAL NOUN

following a Jedi _____ on a top secret _____
                    NOUN   NOUN

or saving a high-ranking _____ from certain doom, the
                             NOUN

work of a clone trooper is demanding and _____. But
                                              ADJECTIVE

there are some bright _____ in the life of a trooper,
                          PLURAL NOUN

including the bond he shares with his fellow _____
                                                 PLURAL NOUN

in arms. They're always there for each other, through thick and

_____. You wouldn't know it looking at them, but
    ADJECTIVE

many clone troopers have a strong sense of _____
                                                NOUN

and are _____ funny. They can make the other soldiers
            ADVERB

_____ so hard that _____ sometimes
    VERB   TYPE OF LIQUID

comes out of their _____!
                       PART OF THE BODY

MAD LIBS® is fun to play with friends, but you can also play it by yourself! To begin with, DO NOT look at the story on the page below. Fill in the blanks on this page with the words called for. Then, using the words you have selected, fill in the blank spaces in the story.

Now you've created your own hilarious MAD LIBS® game!

A BUCKET OF BOLTS

ADJECTIVE _____

NOUN _____

PLURAL NOUN _____

ADJECTIVE _____

VERB ENDING IN "ING" _____

NOUN _____

NOUN _____

PART OF THE BODY (PLURAL) _____

PLURAL NOUN _____

PLURAL NOUN _____

VERB ENDING IN "ING" _____

NOUN _____

NOUN _____

ADJECTIVE _____

PLURAL NOUN _____

A PLACE _____

PART OF THE BODY (PLURAL) _____

MAD LIBS

A BUCKET OF BOLTS

As any _____ pilot will tell you, it's not easy flying
              ADJECTIVE

a space-_____ that's nothing more than a bucket of
              NOUN

_____. Things get especially complicated when you're
   PLURAL NOUN

in the middle of a/an _____ battle and your ship keeps
              ADJECTIVE

_____, putting your _____ in danger.
  VERB ENDING IN "ING"   NOUN

During the Clone Wars, Anakin and Ahsoka flew the *Twilight* in order

to get Rotta the _____ back to his father, Jabba. That
            NOUN

ship was on its last _____. There were dangling
        PART OF THE BODY (PLURAL)

_____ everywhere and the _____ wouldn't
  PLURAL NOUN   PLURAL NOUN

start. Luckily, R2 was able to get it _____. But
              VERB ENDING IN "ING"

when they tried to make the jump into hyper-_____,
              NOUN

they ran into another _____—the ship was too
            NOUN

_____ to hit super-speeds. They had to throw the
  ADJECTIVE

_____ off the ship to make the jump. Fortunately,
  PLURAL NOUN

in the end they made it safely to (the) _____—but only by
            A PLACE

the skin of their _____!
    PART OF THE BODY (PLURAL)

MAD LIBS® is fun to play with friends, but you can also play it by yourself! To begin with, DO NOT look at the story on the page below. Fill in the blanks on this page with the words called for. Then, using the words you have selected, fill in the blank spaces in the story.

Now you've created your own hilarious MAD LIBS® game!

R2 THE HERO

NOUN _____

NOUN _____

ADJECTIVE _____

PLURAL NOUN _____

NOUN _____

PART OF THE BODY _____

VERB ENDING IN "ING" _____

ADVERB _____

VERB ENDING IN "ING" _____

ADVERB _____

NOUN _____

NOUN _____

ADJECTIVE _____

MAD LIBS

R2 THE HERO

R2-D2 might be the feistiest _____ in the galaxy.
                                      NOUN

When he was captured by Gha' Nachkt, he didn't shut down from

fear for even one _____. Instead, he did everything
                           NOUN

he could to destroy Gha' Nachkt's _____ plans to
                                          ADJECTIVE

take all the Republic _____ R2-D2 had stored in his
                          PLURAL NOUN

_____. Even when he was face-to-_____
        NOUN   PART OF THE BODY

with General Grievous himself, R2 made it clear whose side

he was _____ on. And that's not all—he fought
            VERB ENDING IN "ING"

_____ with the double-_____ droid
        ADVERB   VERB ENDING IN "ING"

R3-S6 and won _____! With a loyal droid like R2,
                      ADVERB

it's no wonder Anakin would risk his _____ to
                                            NOUN

get him back to safety. After all, he's more than a droid; he's a good

_____ and a/an _____ companion.
        NOUN   ADJECTIVE

MAD LIBS® is fun to play with friends, but you can also play it by yourself! To begin with, DO NOT look at the story on the page below. Fill in the blanks on this page with the words called for. Then, using the words you have selected, fill in the blank spaces in the story.

Now you've created your own hilarious MAD LIBS® game!

BATTLING ASSASSIN DROIDS, BY AHSOKA TANO

ADJECTIVE _____

PLURAL NOUN _____

PART OF THE BODY _____

NOUN _____

NUMBER _____

ADVERB _____

ADJECTIVE _____

PART OF THE BODY _____

ADJECTIVE _____

NOUN _____

ADVERB _____

VERB _____

ADJECTIVE _____

VERB _____

MAD LIBS
BATTLING ASSASSIN DROIDS,
BY AHSOKA TANO

Assassin droids can be very _____. Once
ADJECTIVE

they've been activated, they'll stop at nothing to kill everything

in their _____. Anakin and I found this out first-
PLURAL NOUN

_____ when we got trapped in a salvage bay
PART OF THE BODY

with two of them on Gha' Nachkt's _____. At first
NOUN

we saw they were deactivated, but that _____-faced
NUMBER

droid, Goldie, _____ powered them up. We were
ADVERB

at a/an _____ disadvantage. Both droids held a
ADJECTIVE

blaster in each _____. Plus, their armor was very
PART OF THE BODY

_____ and Anakin's lightsaber blasts didn't even
ADJECTIVE

make a dent in their _____. In order to stop them,
NOUN

we had to think _____ and _____
ADVERB   VERB

together. Anakin took on one and I took on the other. If you ever

go up against an assassin droid, just remember this—a lightsaber

is more _____ than a blaster. Don't be afraid to
ADJECTIVE

_____ with it.
VERB

MAD LIBS® is fun to play with friends, but you can also play it by yourself! To begin with, DO NOT look at the story on the page below. Fill in the blanks on this page with the words called for. Then, using the words you have selected, fill in the blank spaces in the story.

Now you've created your own hilarious MAD LIBS® game!

GENERAL GRIEVOUS'S GRIEVANCES

NOUN _____

PLURAL NOUN _____

PLURAL NOUN _____

PART OF THE BODY (PLURAL) _____

ADJECTIVE _____

NOUN _____

NOUN _____

ADJECTIVE _____

PLURAL NOUN _____

ADJECTIVE _____

ADVERB _____

NOUN _____

MAD LIBS
GENERAL GRIEVOUS'S
GRIEVANCES

General Grievous, the _____ of the Separatist Army,
　　　　　　　　　　　　　NOUN

doesn't get any respect from his _____, Count Dooku
　　　　　　　　　　　　　　　　PLURAL NOUN

and Darth Sidious. Of course, it doesn't help that he's letting the

Republic _____ slip through his _____.
　　　PLURAL NOUN　　　　　　　　　　　PART OF THE BODY (PLURAL)

He almost had all the Republic's secrets within the _____
　　　　　　　　　　　　　　　　　　　　　　　ADJECTIVE

droid, R2-D2, but he lost him to his arch-_____, Anakin
　　　　　　　　　　　　　　　　　　　NOUN

Skywalker. It seems that _____ is not on his side. As
　　　　　　　　　　　NOUN

Grievous will tell you, the only troops he has are _____
　　　　　　　　　　　　　　　　　　　　　ADJECTIVE

battle droids who would lose their _____ if they
　　　　　　　　　　　　　PLURAL NOUN

weren't literally screwed on. It's a/an _____ life being
　　　　　　　　　　　　　　　ADJECTIVE

General Grievous, but, as he _____ states, "Someone's
　　　　　　　　　　　ADVERB

got to do this _____."
　　　　　NOUN

MAD LIBS® is fun to play with friends, but you can also play it by yourself! To begin with, DO NOT look at the story on the page below. Fill in the blanks on this page with the words called for. Then, using the words you have selected, fill in the blank spaces in the story.

Now you've created your own hilarious MAD LIBS® game!

JAR JAR THE GREAT

NOUN _____

ADJECTIVE _____

VERB ENDING IN "ING" _____

ADJECTIVE _____

NOUN _____

ADJECTIVE _____

PART OF THE BODY (PLURAL) _____

NOUN _____

ADJECTIVE _____

NOUN _____

NOUN _____

NOUN _____

NOUN _____

NOUN _____

ADJECTIVE _____

MAD LIBS

JAR JAR THE GREAT

When Obi-Wan Kenobi and his _____, Qui-Gon Jinn,

NOUN

first met Jar Jar Binks, they didn't know what to think about this

_____-natured Gungan. No matter what situation

ADJECTIVE

they were in or where they were _____, Jar Jar

VERB ENDING IN "ING"

was always making a/an _____ mess of things.

ADJECTIVE

Fortunately, by the time of the Clone Wars, Jar Jar had cleaned

up his _____. When Padmé was captured by the

NOUN

_____ Nute Gunray at the Rodian Consulate, Jar Jar

ADJECTIVE

knew in his heart of _____ that he had to save

PART OF THE BODY (PLURAL)

her. He dressed up as a Jedi _____, fooling everyone

NOUN

into thinking that he had summoned a/an _____

ADJECTIVE

monster from the deep _____. We all need to agree

NOUN

that Jar Jar might be as clumsy as a/an _____ in a/an

NOUN

_____ shop, but when he has something up his

NOUN

_____, you can bet your last _____

NOUN ... NOUN

that something _____ is about to happen!

ADJECTIVE

MAD LIBS® is fun to play with friends, but you can also play it by yourself! To begin with, DO NOT look at the story on the page below. Fill in the blanks on this page with the words called for. Then, using the words you have selected, fill in the blank spaces in the story.

Now you've created your own hilarious MAD LIBS® game!

YODA'S TIPS FOR SPOTTING A DOUBLE AGENT, BY OBI-WAN

ADJECTIVE _____

PART OF THE BODY _____

NOUN _____

PLURAL NOUN _____

NOUN _____

VERB ENDING IN "ING" _____

PLURAL NOUN _____

PART OF THE BODY _____

PLURAL NOUN _____

VERB ENDING IN "ING" _____

NOUN _____

NOUN _____

PLURAL NOUN _____

ADJECTIVE _____

YODA'S TIPS FOR SPOTTING A DOUBLE AGENT, BY OBI-WAN

In these _____ times, it's hard to keep a/an
                ADJECTIVE

_____ on who's a good _____ and who's
PART OF THE BODY   NOUN

not. So if you're like me and you find yourself always scratching your

_____, wondering if the _____ you're
PLURAL NOUN   NOUN

_____ with is a Separatist or with the Republic,
VERB ENDING IN "ING"

remember these three simple rules that Yoda taught me:

1. Always follow your _____ and trust what your
                            PLURAL NOUN

_____ tells you.
PART OF THE BODY

2. Always keep your eyes and _____ open.
                             PLURAL NOUN

3. If you're _____ with someone you don't trust, bring a/
             VERB ENDING IN "ING"

an _____ with you to watch your _____.
     NOUN   NOUN

These double _____ will stop at nothing to capture
                   PLURAL NOUN

a/an _____ member of the Republic.
      ADJECTIVE

MAD LIBS® is fun to play with friends, but you can also play it by yourself! To begin with, DO NOT look at the story on the page below. Fill in the blanks on this page with the words called for. Then, using the words you have selected, fill in the blank spaces in the story.

Now you've created your own hilarious MAD LIBS® game!

PADMÉ'S PARTNERS

PLURAL NOUN _____

PLURAL NOUN _____

ADJECTIVE _____

ADVERB _____

NOUN _____

NOUN _____

NOUN _____

PART OF THE BODY (PLURAL) _____

NOUN _____

TYPE OF LIQUID _____

PLURAL NOUN _____

NOUN _____

ADJECTIVE _____

PART OF THE BODY _____

PADMÉ'S PARTNERS

Going on diplomatic _____ during the Clone
<u>PLURAL NOUN</u>

Wars with Threepio and Jar Jar as my partners was harder than

escaping the vile _____ of Ziro the Hutt or the
<u>PLURAL NOUN</u>

_____ Nute Gunray. Don't get me wrong—I love my
<u>ADJECTIVE</u>

partners _____. But with a/an _____ like
<u>ADVERB</u>   <u>NOUN</u>

Threepio who believes danger lurks around every _____
<u>NOUN</u>

and a/an _____ like Jar Jar who often trips over
<u>NOUN</u>

his own _____, I tried to never let them out
<u>PART OF THE BODY (PLURAL)</u>

of my _____. Whenever I did, they always got into
<u>NOUN</u>

hot _____. If I was gone for more than a few
<u>TYPE OF LIQUID</u>

_____, Threepio was bound to short-circuit. But even
<u>PLURAL NOUN</u>

so, I learned that you can't judge a book by its _____.
<u>NOUN</u>

Those two may not look like your _____ heroes, but they
<u>ADJECTIVE</u>

always come through when I need a helping _____!
<u>PART OF THE BODY</u>

MAD LIBS® is fun to play with friends, but you can also play it by yourself! To begin with, DO NOT look at the story on the page below. Fill in the blanks on this page with the words called for. Then, using the words you have selected, fill in the blank spaces in the story.

Now you've created your own hilarious MAD LIBS® game!

DROIDS, DROIDS, AND MORE DROIDS

VERB ENDING IN "ING" _____

PLURAL NOUN _____

VERB _____

ADJECTIVE _____

NOUN _____

NOUN _____

PLURAL NOUN _____

ADJECTIVE _____

PLURAL NOUN _____

VERB ENDING IN "ING" _____

NOUN _____

ADJECTIVE _____

ADJECTIVE _____

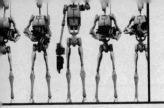

MAD LIBS
DROIDS, DROIDS, AND MORE DROIDS

There are many different kinds of droids _____
                                            VERB ENDING IN "ING"

around during the Clone Wars. Some of them work for the

good _____ while others _____
        PLURAL NOUN   VERB

for the _____ guys. And each droid has a specific
            ADJECTIVE

_____ to perform. For example, assassin droids are
        NOUN

programmed to do one thing and one thing only: destroy every

_____ in their path. Battle droids are always on
        NOUN

the front _____ and the first to engage the enemy.
            PLURAL NOUN

Protocol droids are involved in _____ diplomacy,
                                        ADJECTIVE

searching for peaceful _____ to put an end to the
                            PLURAL NOUN

_____. Astromech droids like R2-D2 help with
VERB ENDING IN "ING"

space-_____ repairs. When all is said and done, it
        NOUN

is important to remember the Clone Wars aren't just about

Republic forces versus Separatist forces, they are also a battle of

_____ droids versus _____ droids!
    ADJECTIVE   ADJECTIVE

MAD LIBS® is fun to play with friends, but you can also play it by yourself! To begin with, DO NOT look at the story on the page below. Fill in the blanks on this page with the words called for. Then, using the words you have selected, fill in the blank spaces in the story.

Now you've created your own hilarious MAD LIBS® game!

COUNT DOOKU'S
DOUBLE DEALINGS

NOUN _____

NOUN _____

ADJECTIVE _____

CELEBRITY _____

LAST NAME _____

NOUN _____

ADJECTIVE _____

ADJECTIVE _____

ADJECTIVE _____

ADVERB _____

PLURAL NOUN _____

ADVERB _____

ADJECTIVE _____

NOUN _____

ADJECTIVE _____

Behind every dastardly _____, every greedy Separatist
NOUN

_____, and all the turmoil of the Clone Wars, is one
NOUN

man—Count Dooku. Once a/an _____ Jedi trained by
ADJECTIVE

none other than Master _____, Dooku turned to the dark
CELEBRITY

side and became Darth _____. Throughout the
LAST NAME

Clone Wars, he tried every trick in the _____ to take power
NOUN

away from the Republic. He even tried to get the _____
ADJECTIVE

Hutts on his side by kidnapping Jabba's _____ son and
ADJECTIVE

trying to place the blame on the _____ Jedi. If his plan
ADJECTIVE

had succeeded and Jabba had _____ joined the Separatists,
ADVERB

there would have been no way the Jedi could win. But in the end,

like all of Dooku's double _____, the plan failed
PLURAL NOUN

_____ and the Jedi emerged the winners. It's too bad
ADVERB

Dooku didn't stay on the _____ side. He might have
ADJECTIVE

come out of the Clone Wars a real _____ instead of
NOUN

a/an _____ loser.
ADJECTIVE

MAD LIBS® is fun to play with friends, but you can also play it by yourself! To begin with, DO NOT look at the story on the page below. Fill in the blanks on this page with the words called for. Then, using the words you have selected, fill in the blank spaces in the story.

Now you've created your own hilarious MAD LIBS® game!

NUTE GUNRAY: A PROFILE IN GREED

NOUN _____

NOUN _____

NOUN _____

ADJECTIVE _____

ADJECTIVE _____

PLURAL NOUN _____

NOUN _____

ADJECTIVE _____

NOUN _____

NOUN _____

PLURAL NOUN _____

NOUN _____

PLURAL NOUN _____

NOUN _____

ADVERB _____

MAD LIBS
NUTE GUNRAY:
A PROFILE IN GREED

Nute Gunray, also known as Viceroy of the _____

                                           NOUN

Federation, will say whatever he needs to get what he wants. As a

business-_____, he's always trying to negotiate the best

                  NOUN

_____ for himself. He doesn't care who gets hurt or

        NOUN

feels _____ as long as he remains _____

          ADJECTIVE   ADJECTIVE

and in charge. Neimoidians, _____ from the planet

                                   PLURAL NOUN

_____ and leaders of the Trade Federation, are known

        NOUN

to be slippery and _____, but Nute Gunray takes

                     ADJECTIVE

this to the next _____. He's always got a trick up his

               NOUN

_____ and can never be pinned down. Even when

        NOUN

he was caught by Republic _____ and put in a/an

                         PLURAL NOUN

_____, he managed to escape. Of course, it didn't hurt

        NOUN

that he has very powerful _____. But someday his

                       PLURAL NOUN

_____ will run out. We can only _____

        NOUN   ADVERB

hope it happens sooner than later.

MAD LIBS® is fun to play with friends, but you can also play it by yourself! To begin with, DO NOT look at the story on the page below. Fill in the blanks on this page with the words called for. Then, using the words you have selected, fill in the blank spaces in the story.

Now you've created your own hilarious MAD LIBS® game!

WHO IS DARTH SIDIOUS?

ADJECTIVE _____

NOUN _____

NOUN _____

NOUN _____

PART OF THE BODY _____

NOUN _____

PERSON IN ROOM _____

ADJECTIVE _____

NOUN _____

TYPE OF LIQUID _____

ADJECTIVE _____

ADJECTIVE _____

NOUN _____

MAD LIBS

WHO IS DARTH SIDIOUS?

In the shadows of the Clone Wars, there lurks an evil and

_____ _____ known only as the Sith
     ADJECTIVE   NOUN

_____, Darth Sidious. Few ever get a chance to meet
     NOUN

this evil master-_____ and even fewer have met
             NOUN

with him face-to-_____. One of the few who has is
         PART OF THE BODY

the Separatist _____ Count Dooku, also known by
            NOUN

his Sith title, Darth _____. But to the majority of us,
           PERSON IN ROOM

what Darth Sidious looks like, where this _____
                ADJECTIVE

_____ lives, even how he takes his morning cup of
     NOUN

_____, are nothing more than _____
   TYPE OF LIQUID   ADJECTIVE

rumors. Only two things are certain—you don't want to cross him

and you definitely don't want to make him _____. If
              ADJECTIVE

you do, your _____ is most certainly in danger.
       NOUN

MAD LIBS® is fun to play with friends, but you can also play it by yourself! To begin with, DO NOT look at the story on the page below. Fill in the blanks on this page with the words called for. Then, using the words you have selected, fill in the blank spaces in the story.

Now you've created your own hilarious MAD LIBS® game!

SKYGUY AND OTHER NICKNAMES

NOUN _____

ADJECTIVE _____

VERB ENDING IN "ING" _____

NOUN _____

ADJECTIVE _____

VERB ENDING IN "ING" _____

ADJECTIVE _____

ADJECTIVE _____

ADJECTIVE _____

NOUN _____

PERSON IN ROOM _____

NOUN _____

PLURAL NOUN _____

ADJECTIVE _____

PART OF THE BODY _____

MAD LIBS

SKYGUY AND OTHER NICKNAMES

Anakin's _____, Ahsoka, has a nickname for everyone.

NOUN

She calls Anakin "Skyguy" not only because of his _____

ADJECTIVE

last name, but because he's so good at _____ through

VERB ENDING IN "ING"

space. She calls Jabba the Hutt's young _____

NOUN

"Stinky" because he smells very _____. If you were

ADJECTIVE

_____ in the Clone Wars with Ahsoka, what would

VERB ENDING IN "ING"

your nickname be? If you were a/an _____ pilot,

ADJECTIVE

perhaps she'd call you "_____ one." If you were

ADJECTIVE

_____ with a light-_____, perhaps

ADJECTIVE   NOUN

she'd call you "_____, the great _____."

PERSON IN ROOM   NOUN

Anakin's gotten so used to Ahsoka's nicknames for all the humans,

droids, and other life-_____ they've met on their

PLURAL NOUN

adventures that he's started using a nickname for her. He calls

Ahsoka "Snips" because she's a little bit _____—

ADJECTIVE

and because she's also got a very sharp _____!

PART OF THE BODY